The Anthology
A Mother's Cry
Volume 1

Visionary Author: Sabrina Young
Co-Authors
Publisher: Nyisha D. Davis
Enga Johnson-Marlow
Darnya Parker/Barber
Shanitha Jones
Carsie Ratliff
Helen Moore
Paula Tuck

ZYIA CONSULTING
Illuminate & Transcend

The Anthology A Mother's Cry: Volume 1

Copyright © 2022 by Sabrina Young

To contact the author, email dcservicingu@gmail.com.

All rights reserved. No portion of this book may be reproduced, stored in a retrieval system, or transmitted in any form or by any means—electronic, mechanical, photocopy, recording, scanning, or other—except for brief quotations in critical reviews or articles, without the prior written permission of the publisher.

ZYIA CONSULTING
Illuminate & Transcend

Zyia Consulting
Book Writing & Publishing Company
www.nyishaddavis.com
nyisha.d.davis@gmail.com

Some names and identifying details have been changed within this book to protect the privacy of the individuals.

Unless otherwise noted, all Scripture quotations are taken from www.blueletterbible.org.

Cover Design: Shalanda Jarbo with Lasting Impressions

ISBN: 978-0-578-29551-0

Printed in the United States of America.

Dedication

I am dedicating this book to all mothers and children across the nation who have experienced some type of hurt or pain due to life's encounters.

Acknowledgment

I would like to acknowledge the following individuals:

- My Pastor, Ralph Gandy, for helping me become the woman I am today.

- Shakira McFadden for motivating me to come forth with what God has in me and for inspiring me to write a book such as this.

- Joan T. Harris for helping me and my children through my cry.

- The women in this book and others who will connect with me and trust me to help them walk in their purpose.

- Last, but not least my children and grands who added to my reason for living.

Visionary Author
Sabrina Young

A New Beginning
Volume 1

TABLE OF CONTENT

Helen's Cry: A Cry For Love 8

Enga's Cry: A Cry for Happiness 14

Darnya's Cry: A Cry for Justice 22

Carsie's Cry: A Cry for Comfort 29

Paula's Cry: A Cry for Courage 40

Shanitha's Cry: A Cry for Peace 44

Nyisha's Cry: A Cry for Clarity 48

Sabrina's Cry: A Cry for Help 56

Author Autograph

Helen's Cry
A Cry for Love

I think back on a song that says, "What's love got to do with it?" Relating to my life and my children, love had everything to do with it. Being deprived of love from my mother, and never being told the three words "I Love you" from her, resulted in me looking for love in a man, drugs, and the streets. This caused me to pass this cycle on to my children. We all began to look for love in all the wrong places.

Supposedly, a mother is to nurture, love, and care for their children. Mothers are known to kiss, embrace, and create a safe environment for their children. But, that was not the case with my mother. I can not remember a day that I felt or heard loving words from her. I began to search for this love. I had a few ladies come through my life that showed me love. However, that did not fill the hole in my heart. Still, at the age of sixty-five-year-old, I have yet to hear her utter those words.

Because my mother did not demonstrate or tell me that she loved me, I began my own journey in the search for love. Instead of making my children my priority and keeping them in a stable household, I allowed my drug addiction to be my first love. This is when I began to pass the cycle on to my children. I left my children with my mother, knowing that the home was without love.

Instead of me breaking the cycle and preventing my children from going through the same things that I did, I began to inflect them with the same wounds that I had. Drugs were my nurturing source. And during this time of my life, that is all I wanted and thought that was all I needed.

Unfortunately, something else grabbed my attention; a man. His grip was even stronger than the drugs. It caused me to abandon my children even more. I remember being so into him, because of the love he was giving me, that I neglected my children for a full year. I can say that I was truly lost in love, not thinking about what my children were enduring. As I think back to when they were little children, I see the pain in their faces.

Not only did they experience the pain of the cycle, but it also affected the way they began to live their lives. Steadily searching for love in a man, resulted in me having four children by the age of twenty. This part of the cycle was passed down to one of my daughters. She had nine children before she was twenty-five from seven different fathers. The search for the love I had for a man manifested in her life.

As for my sons and my other daughter, looking for love in drugs was passed on to them. They lived a life of selling and or using drugs. Not only did drugs cause my family hardship, it caused us a loss. The love for drugs took my baby boy's life. God knows this is not the life that I wanted for my children.

However, the pain continued. I can remember catching charges and going to jail. This same behavior was passed on to my children as well. They began to go in and out of jail like a revolving door. One of my sons did almost fifteen years and my daughter did thirteen years in federal prison. The revolving jail door has been passed on to my grandchildren as well. After many years of incarceration, as of February 2022, my family is finally jail free.

I felt guilty about the cycles that I passed down to my children. Because of my guilt, I began to enable them. I took on raising my daughter's nine children, allowing her to be free to do as she pleased. I allowed my deceased son to manipulate me for money to buy drugs, and it may have resulted in his death. I could not go on carrying guilt and shame of passing on the cycles to my children. I needed freedom.

Finally, I thought about who loved me through it all, Jesus. I realized that His love was all I needed all along. I began to search sincerely and deeply in the things of God. And, that is where I found my true everlasting never-ending love. And, now that I have found him, I will never let go or leave Him. My True Love.

Enga's Cry
A Cry for Happiness

God, is she upset? Is she stiff from screaming so hard? I proceeded to turn the light on. I will never forget. I looked down and saw something coming out of her mouth and nose. I immediately laid her down and ran out of the house, yelling to my sister, "My baby is dead!" I will never forget the look on my baby's face that dreadful morning. This was the beginning of my mother's cry.

My daughter, Kahija, was born as a twin on January 10, 2001. She was home for about a week and a half and passed through the night on February 19, 2001. I thought God would give me a little more time with her. But unfortunately, He saw fit to call His daughter home sooner than later.

I never got a chance to grieve the loss of my daughter. I just kept going like everything was ok, because that is what society had me thinking I needed to do; be strong and move on. What I did not realize is that the feelings and pain did not leave. They were only suppressed. I was walking around like a woman on the outside, but was a battered child on the inside. Who I really was began to show on the day my son was murdered. So, my cry as a mother got more intense.

Loss After Loss

In the month of March 2019, within the same week, I lost my cousin, my son, and my husband lost his uncle. I will never forget it was Sunday, March 10th, I was in Tampa supporting my family on March 11th. I was with my husband and his family during a life and death situation when I got the dreadful phone call that my son had been shot. I passed out for a moment, but then I was finally able to get myself together and make it to the emergency room. While waiting in the emergency room, the doctor came in and told me the worst words in the world, "We did all we could do, but Jabray did not make it."

When I buried my daughter, I went back to work immediately. On Saturday, March 23, 2019, I buried my son and returned back to work two days later. At this time, I was a case manager for youth, and had promised them that I would be there to assist them with obtaining summer employment. And, because I never wanted to disappoint my children I could not disappoint them. I thought I was doing the right thing by going back to work so soon and telling everyone I was ok. But in actuality, I continuously contemplated ending it all.

The death of my children affected me mentally, emotionally, physically, financially, and spiritually. I went into a space that I never imagined. When my daughter passed, I was only twenty-two with five children under the age of five. My daughter, Phashun, was four, Jabray was three, Joe was two and my twins Kahija and Kahari were five weeks old. I tried so hard to prove to everyone I was this superwoman when I was only a woman who needed superpowers.

Suspiciously, on the Thursday before he was murdered, Jabray asked me if I still had life insurance on him. He said that his baby's mom would not be happy until he died. I told him to continue to do what was best for his child, and that is what he did. And, as a result of obeying his mom, he lost his life. I live with the guilt of it every day. I think about the what if's; what if I would have taken the child home or what if I would have told him to just let it go.

I am now dealing with both of my children's deaths at the same time. I was unfamiliar with how to deal with the stages of grief and didn't know what grief meant. I tried to fake to make it, so I would not be judged. I know now that this is not the healthy way to deal with my losses.

A Loss for Many Wins

Looking back over the obstacles that transpired in my life, I know that Jabray's death was not in vain. The obstacles he faced daily to be a father will begin to pave the way for other fathers. It will encourage them to fight for the legal rights to have a relationship with their children, to NEVER exchange custody at a residence, and always meet up at the closest law enforcement agency that the parents agree upon. My son, Jabray, went to take his son to his mom's house to exchange custody. He was murdered in front of his son by the mom's boyfriend and some of his friends.

My prayer is that parents learn that co-parenting is between the mother and father, and all other parties should not get involved, because it only causes issues in the long run. These issues will hurt the child more than any other involved party.

In all ways, I give God all the glory in all the losses that I took. From losing my daughter in 2001, and then in 2019 losing my first cousin, my son, and my uncle in two weeks, to having two car accidents and losing my job. I gained something that I never knew. And, that was Enga, and to learn to love me.

Weaknesses that Became Strengths

I battled with self-esteem issues all my life. From a child until I was forty-two, I never knew what made me happy. If it made another person happy, I would just go with it to keep the peace, but it made my life a living hell. When I tell you that God made my weakness my greatest strength, please believe me. I was never confrontational and would never address the elephant in the room. I allowed people to use and abuse me to keep the peace.

My son's murder investigation is short of being totally blotched. I had to learn how to confront people and sit with people in high places; many with degrees and distinctions. I educated myself to learn the ends and outs of my son's case. This allowed me to shed light on some things that transpired throughout the case.

This fight that I fight is all God. Because of His grace and mercy that reflects in my life, I can have the determination to fight despite the situation that lies before me. I have gained a relationship with God that I never had before and have learned we all have an appointed season. We must be armored for what the season may bring and learn that my blessing is attached to my pressing.

When the shadow of darkness attempts to come up against me, I begin to reflect and say that this too shall pass.

My testimony is going to heal me, and bring someone else through. My family, especially my children, grandchildren and husband deserve for me to fight. They deserve the best Enga that I can be.

Darnya's Cry
A Cry for Justice

Growing Up

Growing up, I was always taught that children were a gift from God. I watched my parents and grandparents thank God for us daily! They helped me to learn this before I ever had children, making it easy for me to understand and accept this when it was my turn. Which by the way came on June 22, 1997!

I gave birth to my first son, Darnell Marquese RayShon Powell! Oh my! He was the most amazing and adorable thing I'd ever seen! I instantly fell in love with him. When he was two months old, I had him christened, at five he was baptized, and eulogized at twenty-one years old.

I Thought I Lost

On September 29, 2018, my son was shot and killed in his sleep. I had never experienced so many questions, pain, hurt, and anger at the same time. I felt betrayed and defeated in every area of my life, especially by God. Was I a bad parent? Did God not trust me anymore? Why couldn't I save him? Did God take him because of my sins?

Everything wrong that I did in my life came back to haunt me. I couldn't pray, go to church, sing, tithe, or do anything else that would please God. My trust was damaged, and my heart was broken. In fact, the only right thing to do was unfortunately the one thing that I'd never imagined having to do; give my child back to God.

Life had really changed for me, at that point. I couldn't trust anyone. No one knew who took my son's life. I didn't know if I was speaking to his killer, the killer's mom or dad, or anyone who had information on my son's death. I didn't trust anyone, especially God. Do you know how many nights I prayed to God to keep him safe and to protect him? Has my Lord fooled me? Did God think I wasn't worthy enough to be his mom? I just didn't know where to run to. I just knew it wasn't to God.

Twenty-one years is half of my age. I've lived two of my son's life terms with lupus, a heart attack, T.I.A., heart surgery, head surgery, four sinus surgeries and a hip replacement. Yet, my healthy loving son was being laid to rest. Leaving me to bury him, instead of him burying me. That's all the time I had; twenty-one years, no college graduation, weddings, grandchildren, or anything coming from him, but pain and misery since he was taken away.

Humbly, on Saturday, October 6, 2018, I had my son's funeral. As hard as it was to hold my head up, I did. I buried my first prince. Grief had moved in and taken residence in my heart. This journey was becoming unbearable. I really felt that God was punishing me for something. I just didn't know what it was. The harder the pain was, the harder my fight was. I was doing everything, but the one thing that God wanted me to do, which was to trust Him again. It wasn't until nine months ago that I had a conversation with my pastor which changed my life forever.

But, I Won

I stood blinded by grief. It had led me to believe that God wanted me to fight this battle alone. I'll never forget telling my pastor that, and he corrected me. "Darnya, that's not true, hunny. God would never give you such a great big job to do by yourself. When you returned him to God, you were supposed to give everything back to God, and wait on Him to get justice for Darnell! All you're supposed to do is wait patiently and faithfully for God to give it to you."

From that point on, I started praying and asking God to forgive me for allowing the loss of my son to cause me to give up on Him! The Lord placed a shield around me throughout the process. My mind changed from feeling like God betrayed me to feeling acceptance and appreciation for every year that I had with him.

I enrolled in a discipleship class to help rebuild my trust in God. From the time I joined, until this very day, the love, peace, and strength I gained along the way were nothing but God-sent. I felt surrounded by a circle of love and sisterhood that I knew I belonged to. It was during that class that it was prophesied to me that losing my son saved my life!! God used him to get your attention. "He needed you, Darnya. Your strength together with your testimony to reach others. He needs your voice."

WOW! That's when I remembered how God allowed the devil to touch Job to test his faithfulness, and then it came together. I wasn't exempt. He needed me to feel this loss and to hear these words so that I can give him the glory by encouraging and reminding other mothers and people everywhere. Although He allowed me to experience such great pain and sorrow, He has never left nor forsaken me.

I was reminded that Darnell was loaned to me by God for twenty-one years. It was time to give God back the child He had given me. I'm so grateful to have been chosen to be Darnell's mom. I thank God for trusting me with him, for allowing me to raise him to be a man. Especially, a man that knew and loved God before us and anything else.

I thank God for the melodies that I hold dear to my heart, and in my head that I remember him singing. I thank God for becoming the woman that I have developed into while raising him. I also thank God for the courage to keep developing, although Darnell is no longer with me.

The easiest thing to do in life is to give up. Especially, when you feel that you control your world and happiness. I don't adjust well to change. I was so used to living my perfectly scheduled life. Every part of life included Darnell so much. Some days, it's so hard to breathe, eat, and swallow. But, I thank God that He allowed my mind to seek more than just "Justice For Dee." He allowed me to find my purpose.

A lot of me died along with Darnell. But, when reality set in that my son is exactly where I'm trying to go when I leave this earth, I stopped being angry with God and learned to trust Him again with myself, my son (Dejon) and every other area of my life. Walking in my purpose allows Him to be glorified. He is truly the only way that I made it through this. I accepted that I had to return and trust God with Darnell, the same way He trusted me.

Carsie's Cry
A Cry for Comfort

I, Carsie Ratliff, was born with a vision to impact and inspire women around the world. I want to share my story with others, so they can see what I've been through and be inspired. With a burning desire to show women that even though you have experienced or are experiencing pain, betrayal, or devastation, there is a way through it. I want you to know that no matter what you've been through or going through you can come out victorious. Your experiences do not end with the cry of your trauma.

As a little girl, I was abandoned by my mother and father. They were rarely in my life. My mother would come around more so than my father. When I saw my father, he would have a thousand excuses why he was not in my life. They would both lie to me, and make promises they never had intentions of keeping.

Abuse of a Mother

My mother was on drugs, and in and out of prison. When she did come around, I watched her steal clothes out of the stores, sell them to get money to feed me and my siblings, and support her drug habits. She would have us living from motel to motel, and always brought different men around us. All they did was drugs, have sex and fight. I can remember my mother being beaten by these same men, stabbing to get them off her. Blood would be everywhere.

At times, I had to be a mother to my siblings, and look after them. Especially, when my mother would get into fights with the men. I would make sure my siblings and I were safe. We would get in the bed, cover up, and put the pillow over our heads so we couldn't hear or see what was going on. My siblings would be so scared and cry. I would hold them and just pray. This was my first mother's cry; mothering my siblings.

I remember a time my mother had to go to court. When she did, she didn't return, because she was sentenced to ten years in state prison. On the day of her court date, a woman police officer came to the motel to get us. She got there just in time. I was bored, and set the room on fire. I was just doing what I saw my mother do when she would smoke crack cocaine on a plate or in a pipe.

The officer removed us from the room and took us to the police station. She put us in a holding cell, and ask me if I had a family member I could call. I called one of my aunties. I'll never forget what she told the police officer when she was asked if she would come get us from the police station. "No! Hell no. They are not my children or my responsibility. You need to call my mother."

I remember the policewoman had tears in her eyes. She asked my auntie, "Ma'am, you mean to tell me, you won't come get your own sister's children? Your own flesh and blood?" My aunt told her, "I told you no. And, I'm telling you again they are not my children, and I'm not coming to get them. Call my mother who is their grandmother."

Emotionally she called my grandmother, and my grandmother didn't exchange words. She came and picked us up, took us home, and bathe and fed us fish and grits. I remember that like it was yesterday. She raised us until we were grown. Thank you, grandma. No little girl or child should've had to witness or go through any of that.

My grandmother raised me well. But, she never told me she loved me or expressed how proud she was of the accomplishments that I made until I got older. To include, I experienced verbal abuse from a family member. They would tell me you are nothing, you aren't going to be nothing and you are going to be just like your crackhead mother. They would use profanity while saying these things to me. They even told me that my grandmother only took me and my siblings in to get welfare and food stamps.

These things were said to me often, especially after I got pregnant and had my baby at fourteen. This same family member told me my life was over. And, at one point, I believed them. Unfortunately, I lost my grandmother two years after my mom passed. My mom passed due to drugs.

Abuse of a Father

At the age of thirteen, I was molested and lost my virginity to my father. My father was the first man to break my heart. Being molested by him was hurtful, painful, and devastating. From then on, I dealt with low self-esteem. I didn't feel pretty or good enough or worthy at times. I would question myself and ask God the whys. Why did my father do this to me? Why did my mother abandon me? Why weren't they good parents to me? Why didn't they love me? I also asked, what did I do so bad to deserve this? I didn't ask to be here. I didn't choose them to be my parents. All I wanted was love and wanted to be loved.

I became so angry at the world. I hated myself for quite some time. I was bullied, and then the bully which resulted in me getting cut. I had to get more than a hundred stitches over my body. I almost died. But, God! It's only by the grace of God that I'm still alive, and that I didn't turn to drugs and become a crackhead like my mother. At one point, I did try cocaine, however, God had better plans for my life.

The Wrong Love

Wanting the love from my father that I never got, I began to look for love in all the wrong men, choosing one bad man after another. Yes, men became my weakness. So, every man that came into my life I would give them a chance, thinking they loved me only to allow myself to be abused and used. Believing every lie and tolerating their bad behavior, because I thought that's what love was supposed to feel like. All I really wanted was just to be loved.

A Reason to Live

Finally, I asked God and my first child's father to give me a baby so I could feel loved. I thought if I had a baby, that baby would love me, fill that void that was missing in my life, and give me a reason to live. My first child saved my life. I felt like I had a reason to live. I dropped out of school somewhere between the ages of fourteen and fifteen to take care of my first baby.

I didn't want to live off of welfare or raise my baby in a government project. So, I got a job, and later got my high school diploma. I became pregnant again with my second child at the age of seventeen. A single mother with two children by different men. However, that did not stop me. I worked hard and bought my first home for me and my two children at the age of nineteen. I was a mother to my children that my mother wasn't to me. That's my second mother's cry.

The Many Losses

My husband and I got married at the age of twenty, and he passed ten years later. I got so angry at God for taking my mother, grandmother, and now my husband. That was three deaths back to back. I walked away from God and the church, and became an alcoholic until I almost lost my life drinking and driving.

During our marriage, my husband cheated on me three times with the same woman. I became bitter and hated all women who would have an affair with married men, until I became one of those women. Yes, God will allow the devil to test you. The result of that is that my third and last child is from a married man. Who would have ever thought I would have a baby from a married man. I wanted to kill myself. I was so ashamed, humiliated and embarrassed. I never thought or wanted this to be a part of my book of life. But, God!

The Cry

While I was married, my baby boy was molested by my stepson. Immediately, I put my stepson out of the house. He was to never return to my home. I took my son to the hospital and he received the care he needed. I got him spiritual counseling, but I regret not getting him professional counseling. I did not think he would remember what had happened to him, because he was so young. I thought spiritual counseling would be enough for him, but I was so wrong. I should have gotten my son the proper help/counseling that he needed, because this has impacted his life tremendously.

Our relationship is not the best. We do not see eye to eye. He blames me for him being molested and the reason why he lives an alternative lifestyle. When this took place, I didn't know what was going on with my son or in my home. I was working, attending to my sick husband who was always in and out of the hospital and at doctor appointments due to him having sickle cell. I was being a mother, trying to hold the house down, and be a superwoman.

I've apologized to my son so many times for what happened to him and for neglecting his need for professional help. I've always reassured him that it wasn't his fault. If I could rewind time and take it back, I would. My prayer is that, one day, my son and I would reconcile spiritually and get through this together. I truly love him with everything in me.

The Cry's Glory

I don't wish this pain or hurt on him, myself or anyone. I want to be a part of the fight against this type of pain. No little girl, boy, woman, or man should have to go through these situations. I want people to know that they do not have to go through it alone. I also want my story to uplift, impact, and touch every broken little girl and woman to let them know it wasn't or is not their fault, and to let them know they are good enough. When God made you, He made no mistake and you were born with purpose.

God will always get the glory out of my testimony and life, because I know I went through all of that for a reason. God will use me in a great way to shine light and hope on His children. Like I've told my children before, I became so they could become. What I've been through did not kill me, but it only made me stronger and better. To God be the Glory. Amen.

Paula's Cry:
A Cry for Courage

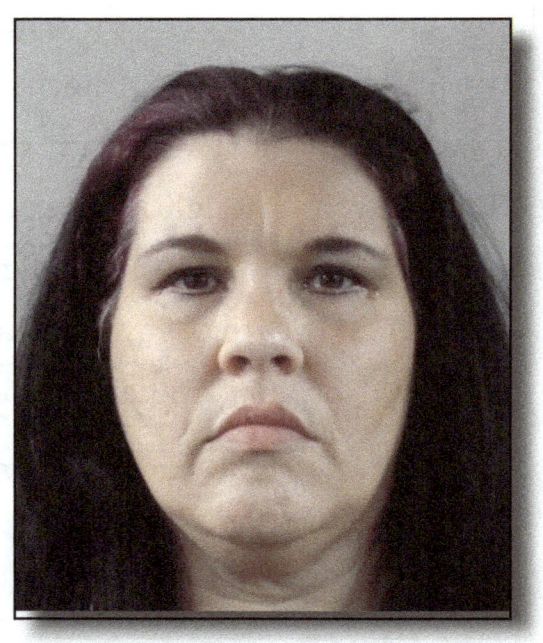

This random day in June 2006 changed my life forever. That morning, we woke up and it was like any other day. I got the children in the bathtub, and got them ready for the day. Disaster hit. My eleven-month-old daughter was in the tub with her three-year-old brother. I stepped away for just a few minutes. She fell and hit her head. This caused bleeding in her brain. I came back in to find her not breathing. I called 911 and performed CPR until the ambulance got there.

For three long days, my family prayed, cried, and drove back and forth to Tampa General Hospital. My mom sat vigil with her in the hospital room, read books, and played her favorite videos. I was not able to hold my little girl or sing to her. I cried constantly. I could not be a mother to her, because the Department of Children and Family had a court order that stated that neither my husband nor I could be alone with our children.

Hard Decision & Hard Times

On June 7, 2006, my husband and I made the hardest decision of our lives to let our little girl go. I've never been the same. I had nightmares and doubts about myself as a person and a mother. I was mad and felt betrayed, and I lost all faith. I blamed God for taking my innocent little girl. Why my baby girl? Why my family? Why me?

We buried our baby girl, Alexus Helana Eliana, on June 12, 2006. I lost everything. I faced criminal charges six months later. They arrested me, charged me with child neglect, and sentenced me to fifteen years of probation. My life has been a roller coaster ever since. My drug abuse spiked, and I went on a two year binge. All I wanted to do was smoke dope and not deal with or feel any of the pain. As a result, my family lived in chaos all the time.

Found My Way

It took a long time for me to come back to God. I finally found my way back to Him in 2013, when I got the guts to leave my abusive marriage and start over with another man. This man saved my life. He got me away from an abusive relationship and twice saved me from two intentional overdoses. A year later, my son, Logan, was born. He again was a lifesaver. He is one of the main reasons I love God so much. His birth was an expression of God's love to me. I finally came to know my Savior, our Lord.

God has been my strength while I've been to prison, rehab, and in jail. But, I am in recovery fighting to keep my life one day at a time. So, just for today, I am okay. Let's see what tomorrow brings. I don't cry nearly as much as I used to. I read my Bible daily and thank God for all my blessings. Only by His grace, I am nearly five months sober and still alive today to write this testimony. He held me up when I was tired, and walked this long journey back to sanity with me. So, now I will share my testimony with others who may have the same or similar encounters of life so that God will get the glory. As of today, I am proud to call myself a Christian and a recovering addict.

Shanitha's Cry
A Cry for Peace

    Inspired to be a rapper, Dyreon, my oldest son, was murdered at the age of nineteen years old. He worked at our local funeral home and took care of his elderly aunt. Dyreon's real passion was football. However, he became ill in 2020 and had to give up the game he loved so much.

He Is Mine

On the fateful morning of Sunday, May 23rd, I called and spoke with my son about this show called "For Life." That's what we did. If it was a show he watched and thought I'd like, he'd call to tell me about it, and I would do the same. Around 12:30 p.m., while I was doing hair, I received the phone call that changed my life forever. I was told that my son had been shot, and I needed to come to the hospital A.S.A.P. I instantly started calling his phone, only not to get an answer. When told by the police to go to the hospital, I started praying, crying, and calling my family.

When I arrived at the hospital, there were police and people everywhere. I was later told that my son had been shot in the head. I lost it. It's like my world had ended. Due to his injury, they transferred him to a hospital that had a trauma unit. When I arrived, I got the news that he died. I think I passed out three or four times. I became very angry, bitter, and just wanted to end it all.

One day, I was on the phone telling a lady that they

took my baby from me and how he was mine. I was just running my mouth. As I was talking, I heard God speak and say, "He was mine. I breathed breath in his body. I gave him to you. He was mine." It's like everything left me. Anger and bitterness were gone. The feeling of wanting to die left. However, the hurt was still there.

At Dyreon's funeral, there was nothing but love. We were in the middle of the pandemic and there were people everywhere. Nobody had anything bad to say about my son. I gained strength from the love that everyone gave during this loss, and was able to stand up and sing a song at my son's funeral. So, if you are experiencing a lot or encountering a tragedy, try to look around and gain strength from something or someone.

It Works For the Good

My eighteen-year-old son, Zee, thinks highly of my son Dyreon, and looked up to him as a father figure, even an idol. Since his brother's death, Zee has been arrested and charged with crimes that I believe he's innocent of. While being incarcerated, my son says that God comes and talks to him. I explained to him that God removed his brother (idol) and placed him in isolation to talk to him, to show him who should be first in his life. When he was in the streets, he didn't have time for Him or acknowledge Him.

From all that my son experienced in 2021, he said that he now knows without a doubt God is real. Parents and children were hurt, lost and angry for many reasons. As a result of my son's death, it caused a lot of confusion and chaos within my community. However, the tragedy that happened to him can help others; parents of young men being murdered can come together to show children we can get alone to get along. And, that there is more to life than the streets. If we could set aside our emotions, pain and hurt, and live peacefully amongst one another as much as we could, through this God will get all the glory.

Nyisha's Cry
A Cry for Clarity

    I could take this time and talk about the many natural cries that I have had as a mother. However, I believe that it is more important for me to focus on the spiritual cries that I have endured and are glorifying God. I am a mother of one son, Ja'Quez RaeShard Thomas. He is twenty-two years old, at this time. He is my one and only blessing of my womb. Believe me, God knew what I could handle; one child. I was chosen and trusted by The Creator to be a mother to him; to train him up in the way that he should go so that when he got older he would not depart from it. (Proverbs 22:6)

I raised my son with every intention of not controlling him and giving him everything that I did not have growing up. I did not want him to ever think of me in a negative light. I did everything I thought was good for him, so that he would love and thank me all of his days. There were times in his life that I knew that I could have been more stern and disciplined. But, I was so focused on making sure that I was not trying to control his life, so I dismissed important principles of raising him.

After Ja'Quez entered his twenties, the enemy try to make me believe that I was not a good mother, because I did not do everything "right." The enemy once told me that I failed my son. My spirit spoke back to it and said, "I did not create him, so I cannot fail him." The Holy Spirit was always there/here to comfort me with His words, "If I wanted you to do something different, I would have made sure of it. I know what is required for Ja'Quez's journey. His journey required him not to have everything you wanted him to have, but to have everything that I wanted and needed him to have." That gave me so much peace.

God is In Control

Trying not to control his life and give him more freedom than I had, God still showed me that He was in control of his journey. I want you to see how the power of God's control has worked so much in his life, even before he was born! The enemy planned to take him out before he was born by wrapping his umbilical cord around his throat and leg. The enemy did not win, because he was born healthy, in his right mind, has a voice, and still moving forward in life.

I gave Ja'Quez to my mother to raise when he was eighteen months old. I was on drugs and doing everything that I wanted to do. His biological father abandoned him. Once I committed my life to Christ, my son came to live with me. He was six years old at the time. God blessed him with not a stepfather but a father who stepped in and loves him not "like a son," but because Ja'Quez is his one and only son.

I remembered praying every day while I was pregnant, because I didn't want my baby to be ugly and get picked on as I was growing up. Unfortunately, he was still made to feel ugly throughout his adolescent years, even though he was just as beautiful as he was shown to me in my dream. During his middle school and high school years, the enemy's plan was to destroy him with depression to try to influence him to kill himself. Even after having had guns pulled on him, on two different occasions, while he was trying to protect his friends that he loved, he is still alive today.

Connivingly, the enemy's plan was to kill him by using

his protective love that he had for another. I got a call at 2:30 a.m. on Sunday, May 20, 2018. Ja'Quez had been hit by a car. I then took a moment to reflect back to when he was fourteen years old, I found out that he and his friend had stolen my car while I sleep. After I finished talking to him and he was given his punishment, I walked to my bedroom. As I got into bed, I asked God, with an attitude, "Why didn't you wake me up?" He replied to me sternly, "I didn't need to wake you up." Then the peace surpassed all my understanding came upon me, and I laid down knowing my Father was in control. Remembering this moment, I found clarity in knowing that God had him even after he had been hit by the car.

Gratefully, he is still alive and a walking talking miracle after four months in the hospital, learning how to function all over again. Looking at him, you would never know that he had part of his skull removed to allow room for his brain to swell, or that he had four major surgeries on his head just to save his life. The glory of God sits and rests on him.

Even now, the enemy's plan is to persuade him to believe the false truths about himself and his life's purpose. Nevertheless, the Word of God will not return to Him void. Ja'Quez comes in the full volume of the book that God has written of him in Heaven. Ja'Quez is God's Word. God is in control and His promises are still "Yes" and "Amen." (2 Corinthians 1:20)

Cries for Clarity

Through the trials of my life, as a mother, I learned that if I cry in prayer out of my emotions nothing was going to happen. My flesh was crying, not my spirit, so nothing would transpire in the spirit realm. The cries from our spirits open spiritual doors, unclog spiritual channels, release angels to ascend and descend, and release warring angels to fight for our children's life purposes. These cries manifest through praise and worship!

I had to learn that my cries could not be self-driven,

only Spirit-driven. Some people say that I am too calm or too unconcerned in the way I move concerning my son. But, when the Lord shows you how He wants you to move as a mother and who your son is in the spirit, you will make the choice to trust Him.

As mothers, we are not to move as the world tells us to move with control and manipulation to get our children to function as we want, to keep us from living in worry. We are to be mothers by the Spirit of God, to cry and release prayers over our children through the Word of God. I want to encourage you to cry from your spirit and stop crying from your flesh. Yes, I know that every son and daughter has a life journey that is different from my son's. But, what I know to be true is that God's plans for our children are nowhere near what we have made up in our minds.

Holy Spirit taught me, through each of my son's trials, that He had a plan for him. I had to accept that every trial, every negative event, every turmoil that my son has had, is having and will go through is for the pressing of the oil for his anointing that God has given to him. God trusts him with his anointing, so who am I to stop what God needs for him to go through? I will not understand everything, but I will accept what God has purposed for him.

God will get the glory when we allow His Spirit to lead us in prayer for our children. We must move out of the way to allow our children to get to Jesus. "But Jesus said, Suffer little children, and forbid them not, to come unto me: for of such is the kingdom of heaven." Matthew 19:14

Sabrina Young
A Cry for Help

Saying April Showers bring May flowers was definitely not just a cliche for me. Noticing, for the past five years in the month of April I would encounter some type of loss or setback. I'm not sure how many years this seemingly cursed cycle had been going on. However, it caught my attention more so in the year 2006, when not only did it rain it poured. The loss of my mom in January, the abortion in March, and then the incarceration which lead to the separation of me and my children in the month of April. This was not only a shower, but A Mother's Cry.

A Mother's Loss

What a way to start the new year. Losing my mom unexpectedly was devastating. One of the most devastating things about it is that she gave us a warning that we didn't take heed to. As I think back on the day she cried out to me, and said she needed to go to the hospital I did not believe her. She would often go just to get the prescription medication. My mom was addicted to street and prescribed drugs. She would substitute the prescription to prevent herself from using street drugs.

She battled with this addiction most of my life. I somewhat began to model after her lifestyle in my early teenage years. Although my mom didn't raise me, somehow this cycle was passed down to me. Fighting, drugs, stealing, cunning and living the street life were many of the things I picked up.

However, this last time in January 2006, when she cried out for medical attention, I didn't realize that in this month this would be one of her last cries. Days later, she had the hospital reach out to us and inform the family that it was an emergency and we needed to come to see her immediately. Just to get up there and see her sitting on a portable toilet smiling big as the joker as she told us it was only a prank, because she wanted somebody to come to see her. Well, a few days later, her prank became her truth. She died from congestive heart failure at the age of forty-nine years old. This may not have been my first cry as a mother, but my mother's cry caused my cry, as a mother, to be stronger and longer.

Somehow, I knew I had to get to a place where I could cope and focus after the loss of my mom. At this time, I was a single mother of five. I had a nine, seven, two, one year old, and also a two and a half-month-old. I tried to get through the loss of my mother the best I could. The struggle became harder when I found out, on Valentine's Day, that I was pregnant with baby number six.

The Unborn Abuse

My two-year-old and the other two younger siblings were still in diapers. I had never learned to potty train, because when my two older children were infants I spent most of my time in and out of jail. I never had anyone to help or guide me through my parenthood. With no family or moral support, I had to try to learn on my own. However, this was not an easy task. I just thought it was unbearable with being pregnant again.

I was still married, but had been separated for about two years at this point. Even though my husband and I each had a baby with other partners during this separation, I still had hopes that we would reunite and raise our family, including the outside children.

Unfortunately, my husband had other plans. We both were on our second outside child. He was incarcerated, but was in a whole relationship with another woman with whom he was on baby number two with. I was on my second outside the marriage baby with a second man. This was just a whole mess. Yet, I still felt like God was going to fix it for us in some way, somehow. I wanted my marriage to work along with not wanting to have four children in diapers alone.

I felt as if the abortion was the best thing for me. Hypocritically, I was one who was against and sometimes judged those who had abortions. I felt as if no circumstance or situation should cause someone to kill an unborn child. Well, I had to eat the words. The word of God says, "Judge not, that ye be not judged." (Matthew 7:1) Judgment was now against me.

I forced the father of this unborn child to pay for the abortion. If you ask how I forced him, I literally physically abused him and told him I would do it every day, sometimes all day, until I got tired if he didn't pay for it. He rebelled against the decision and tried to avoid it. Until one day, he got tired of the verbal and physical abuse, along with not wanting to see me go to jail, and he honored my wishes.

The abuse didn't stop there. Not only did I physically and verbally abuse him, I mentally abused him by making him drive me there, go in the room with me, and watch them abort our unborn child. He was hurt and said he would never forgive me for this. I wouldn't blame him. I don't think I ever forgave myself up until this day.

Today, I look at my other five children, and I feel incomplete. I feel as if there will always be avoid. I ask God daily to allow me to see him or her in a dream, a mirage or something. I will always look for Oshae. That is the name I gave the child. A mutual name whether it is a girl or a boy. I felt like that name would suit. I know if I can't see him or her on this side I will definitely see him or her on the other side in Heaven. Because, all babies go to Heaven, and I am striving to make it in.

The Case

To add, I forgot about the situation I was dealing with in December 2005. I had spanked, or shall I say whipped, my second oldest for cutting her brother's hair to the skull. I did not only spank her for doing this. I spanked her for lying and saying she did not do it. In my family, we value honesty. My grandma would tell us it's better to tell the truth, because if you get caught in a lie you get punished worse.

The punishment from the older generation seemed fair, but it was severe. We got whipped with whatever they could get ahold of. What today deems to be child abuse, is what our ancestors deemed a whooping. Nevertheless, once again, I modeled the modern ways that I had been taught and that is how I felt I should try and raise my children. What I was taught is what I was teaching.

Although it was done this way, it does not mean it was

right. See, our ancestors could have still been damaged by modern-day slavery. So, they may have affected the generation after with what they knew. However, this mindset that was passed on to me caused me to encounter some hardships.

This same year, the state of Florida had just passed a law that spanking with a belt was a weapon. To add, if the child obtained a welp the person who used the belt would be charged. I had done both. Not only did I do that. I had attempted to smack her in the mouth for lying. I was taught, if you lie out the mouth, you get hit in the mouth. But, instead, I caught the side of her face due to her doing the whooping dance. This mistake opened a door to pain, but change.

The school called the Department of Children and Family (DCF) and reported me. The DCF investigator came out along with the police and got my statement. They said if they had any more questions they would come back. They later came back and said they would monitor me for a couple of months. I had to complete a few in-home parenting classes, and was told not to get in any trouble while the case was open, and then it would be settled.

I thought it was a typical investigation. I believed they would know it was just a single mom trying to raise a child and discipline them for something wrong they did, and this little situation would go away. However, that was not the case. This was a case that I later found out was an ongoing investigation.

What Am I to Do?

Unknowingly, April 6th would be another one of the worst days of my life. You would think I have had enough painful encounters by now. But, I guess I would never be able to write this testimony if I had not gone through all I had. It was another stressful day for me, having three in diapers, and exhausted all of my community resources as well as cash assistance. Then to add to it all, I had a sanction on my food stamps due to not complying or being able to comply with the welfare program. The noncompliance meant no help with childcare. This resulted in not being able to work. I was in a jam that I felt only I could get myself out of, just to get myself in a worse one.

I was out of food, had no diapers, and had no family support. What's a girl to do? I had turned to all I knew. If nobody gave me what I wanted and needed, or if I couldn't work for it, I would go shoplifting and take it. And, that is what I did. Out of all the times I got by, this day, I did not.

I went to Dollar General with a couple of my family members and filled my buggy up with all the things we needed at home; food, diapers, etc. I walked out the door. A good citizen saw me and informed the clerk. The clerk pursued me. Well, I was very desperate so I kept going.

The police were called. I tried to get away, but the direction I went in, I ran right into the police. We were captured and taken into custody. Not to mention, I was already on probation for stealing. So, this incarceration lead to a violation of probation.

My children were at school. When they got home, they found out mama would not be there and not for some time. Painfully, I sat in jail worried about my children. I didn't know when I was going to be able to go home. I did not know what was going to happen to my children, because I violated probation.

I found out, when I got a visit from the DCF caseworker, that my children were with a friend of the family. They were with a guy I admired and his mother; my neighbors at the time. His mother would get the children, because no one in my family would or could get them. This gave me some type of comfort. I felt as if she was more than capable of caring for them.

Just when I thought I could focus on just getting out of jail, they call me out of my cell just to tell me that I would be getting additional fingerprints and charged with child abuse, because of the incident from December with my daughter. Could things get any worse? I am sure they could have. I did not understand why all this was happening to me. All my mind could think of was all the wrong things I had done; the abortion, committing adultery, having an outside baby, the stealing, and more.

All of this was impacting my thoughts. I knew it was time for a change, a real change. And, I knew that God was the only one to help me through. So, I cried out to Him with a broken heart and a contrite spirit, knowing He would answer me. This pain was a different kind of pain.

Win! Win! Win!

Yes, it hunted me to lose my mom and kill an unborn child. But, the loss of my living children affected me the most. I don't think it was a day that went by that I did not cry. During this time, they constantly moved from one placement to another. I wasn't sure how things were going to turn out. I heard the different stories from the women in jail about how they or some of their children went to foster care and got molested and or abused sexually, physically and verbally. My heart hurled severely just from the thought.

This caused me to get closer to God. I knew He was the only one that had the power to control this situation. It was out of my hands. I knew not only did this situation need to change. I had to for the better and good for the sake of myself and my children.

I knew I never in life wanted to be away from them and experience this pain again. I had to make some vows with God and remember His word said it is better not to make a vow than to make one and break one with God. (Ecclesiastes 5:5) I wasn't afraid though. I knew it was no turning back.

Fortunately, during the incarceration and separation, I saw some good in it. I was able to build my relationship with God and it got stronger and deeper. While doing so, I was able to help other women in the jail build their relationships with Christ. I lead Bible study and prayer circles, on a daily basis, in the cell. I attended the church services every time I could in there. I thank God that I did.

I remember when my children were headed to foster care from the previous caregiver. The caregiver no longer wanted to care for them. I almost lost faith. One night, I went to church, and God sent me an angel. It was Mrs. Joan T. Walker a.k.a. "Jan Harris" known for being in jail. She had changed her life after so many years of incarceration. Jan Harris was now back in the jail on the other side ministering to women that were in the same condition she was in. This was my hope and inspiration. She reached out to a member of her church to get the children and keep them from staying in foster care. I was so thankful and always feel in debt to her.

I am fifteen years of being jail free. I am truly dedicated to God. I now go back to the jail and teach parenting classes to women. Jan Harris inspired me in such a way that I want to inspire women, until the day God calls me home.

To conclude, April showers did bring May flowers. All that I encountered caused me to be all that I am today. I want to give honor and glory to our Heavenly Father,

God Almighty. It is only because of Him that I was able to go through and get through what I encountered in this month of April 2006. The loss of my mom, abortion, and incarceration that led to me and my children's separation is all a part of why I am writing my testimony in the month of April 2022, sixteen years later.

I will forever be grateful for this change that God has brought about in my life. I will tell the story that He may continuously get the glory out of my life. I will forever encourage other women and help them through their process to tell their story that God may get the glory out of their lives. The only way that we may overcome and beat the enemy is by the blood of the lamb and the word of our testimony. (Revelation 12:11)

References

Britten, T., Kygo, Lyle, G. (1984). What's Love Got to Do with it. [Tina Turner]. What's Love Got to Do with It. New York City, New York. Parlophone.

Jackson III, C. J., Steinberg, H., Robinson, D., (Producers) & Benigni, R., Busfield, T., Fine, R. L., Steinber, H. (Directors). (2020). For Life. ABC Studio.

ZYIA CONSULTING
Illuminate & Transcend

www.ingramcontent.com/pod-product-compliance
Lightning Source LLC
Chambersburg PA
CBHW071841290426
44109CB00017B/1890